I'M ALLERGIC TO...

Wheat

Written by E.C. Andrews

KidHaven PUBLISHING

Published in 2025 by
KidHaven Publishing, an Imprint of
Greenhaven Publishing, LLC
2544 Clinton St., Buffalo, NY 14224

Written by: E.C. Andrews
Edited by: Rebecca Phillips-Bartlett
Designed by: Jasmine Pointer

Cataloging-in-Publication Data

Names: Andrews, E.C.
Title: Wheat / E.C. Andrews.
Description: Buffalo, NY : KidHaven Publishing, 2025. | Series: I'm allergic to… | Includes glossary and index.
Identifiers: ISBN 9781534549104 (pbk.) | ISBN 9781534549111 (library bound) | ISBN 9781534549128 (ebook)
Subjects: LCSH: Food allergy--Juvenile literature. | Food allergy in children--Juvenile literature. | Wheat--Juvenile literature.
Classification: LCC RJ386.5 A53 2025 | DDC 616.97'5--dc23

Manufactured in the United States of America

CPSIA compliance information: Batch #CW25KH
For further information contact Greenhaven Publishing LLC at 1-844-317-7404.

Please visit our website, www.greenhavenpublishing.com.
For a free color catalog of all our high-quality books, call toll free 1-844-317-7404 or fax 1-844-317-7405.

Find us on

Image Credits

All images are courtesy of Shutterstock.com. With thanks to Getty Images, Thinkstock Photo and iStockphoto.

Cover – judyjump, Jiri Her, Nataly Studio, Olga Selyutin, Oliver Hoffmann, Sergio33, ShotPrime Studio, Spalnic, Ysami, subkontr, Vector Bakery. Throughout – judyjump. 4–5 – marilyn barbone, onstockphoto. 6–7 – Sorapop Udomsri, Galigrafiya, Lo-Random. 8–9 – Ievgenii Meyer, Julia Lav, SMDSS, Victoria Sergeeva. 10–11 – Pixel-Shot, aperturesound, Best_photo_studio, Sergiy Kuzmin. 12–13 – onstockphoto, Infomages, K-D-uk. - Sam Lee. 14–15 – Diana Taliun, Moving Moment, Andrii Horulko, P Maxwell Photography. 16–17 – fizkes, Brent Hofacker, Hong Vo, Luis Echeverri Urrea, NIKCOA. 18–19 – Tukaram.Karve, Imageman, Spalnic, M. Unal Ozmen, Yulia Gust. 20–21 – Viktory Panchenko, Africa Studio, MaraZe, bigacis, Dionisvera. 22–23 – Evgeny Atamanenko, MarinaMos.

Contents

Words that look like **THIS** can be found in the glossary on page 24.

Delicious Diets

Your diet is made up of all the foods that you usually eat. It is important to eat each food in the right amount for our bodies. This is called eating a balanced diet.

Some people cannot eat certain foods. This might be because of an allergy. Allergies can make eating a balanced diet feel tricky. However, there are still plenty of other healthy foods to try.

What Is an Allergy?

An allergy is when your body has a bad **REACTION** to something that is usually harmless. This happens because your body mistakes this thing for something harmful.

People can be allergic to all kinds of things. Allergic reactions can make you feel very sick. Some allergic reactions are more serious than others. Being allergic to wheat is very common.

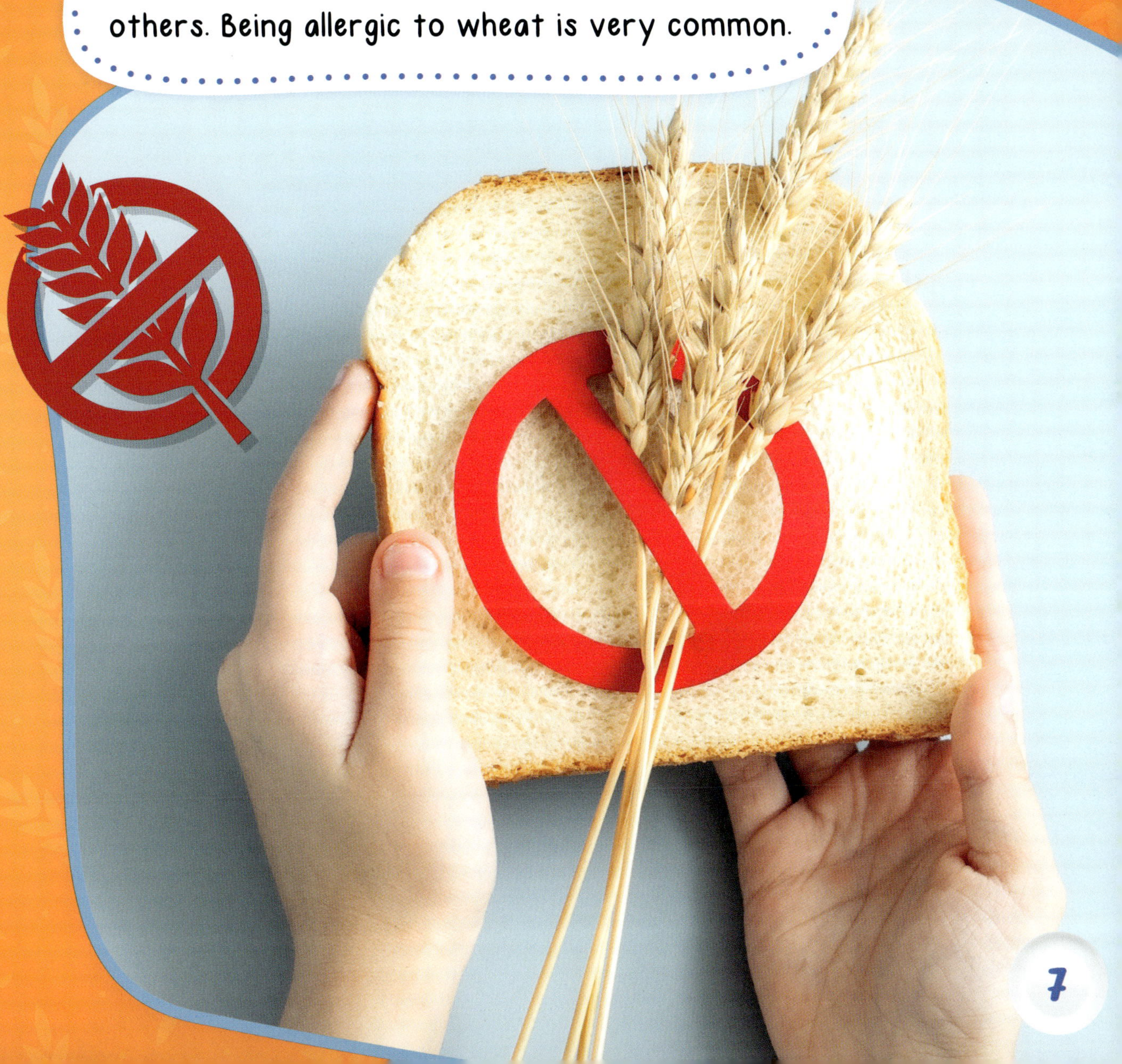

What Is Wheat?

Wheat is a type of grass. Humans grow wheat for its seeds. Wheat seeds are a type of grain. Wheat is used as an **INGREDIENT** in different foods.

A lot of the flour we use is made from ground-up wheat grains. There are different kinds of wheat flour. Whole wheat flour is made with **WHOLE GRAINS**. White flour has a lot of the whole grains taken out.

What Are Wheat Products?

Foods such as bread, cookies, and cakes are often made using wheat flour. Wheat flour is also used to make pasta. But wheat is not just in things made with flour.

Wheat can be found in sauces, breakfast cereals, and even some meat products, such as hot dogs. People with wheat allergies should avoid foods with labels that say:

Symptoms of a Wheat Allergy

If you feel ill after eating wheat, talk to a grown-up. A wheat allergy could cause these **SYMPTOMS**:

- **Headache**
- **Blocked nose**
- **Trouble breathing**
- **Itchy skin**
- **Feeling or being sick**
- **SWELLING or itching of the mouth and throat**

Anaphylaxis is a dangerous allergic reaction. An autoinjector **INJECTS** medicine that helps with anaphylaxis. If you have been given an autoinjector, it is important to always carry it with you.

After using your autoinjector, call 911 right away.

Smart Swaps

You can still bake delicious things if you are allergic to wheat. There are many different types of flour that are completely wheat-free. Buckwheat flour, quinoa flour, and millet are great choices.

Flour can be made from some nuts and seeds. Almond meal is made from ground-up almonds. Ground flaxseed can be sprinkled over food to make it extra tasty. It can also be used for baking.

Nut flours can add a delicious nutty taste to your food.

Super Starch

Starch is a type of **CARBOHYDRATE**. It gives your body enough **ENERGY** to work. Starch is an important part of a balanced diet. Starch can be found in wheat products.

Starch can also be found in lots of wheat-free foods. Potatoes are a **SOURCE** of starch that can be cooked in many different ways. Starchy powders made from arrowroot and tapioca make great baking flours.

Wheatless Bread

To make a lovely loaf of wheat-free bread, you will need:

- 15 ounces of oats
- 16 ounces of plain yogurt
- 1 handful of buckwheat flour
- 1 handful each of sunflower, pumpkin, and sesame seeds
- 1 teaspoon of baking soda
- 10 teaspoons of olive oil

Some oats and seeds may have traces of wheat in them. Remember to check the labels.

Let's cook!

- Heat your oven to 350 degrees Fahrenheit (180 degrees Celsius).
- Mix the yogurt, oats, and baking soda together.
- Rub your baking pan with the olive oil. Then, lightly sprinkle it with buckwheat flour.
- Pour your mixture into the baking pan. Sprinkle sunflower, pumpkin, and sesame seeds on top.
- Bake in the oven for 40 to 45 minutes. Enjoy!

Chunky Chocolate Cookies

To make some wonderful wheat-free cookies, you will need:

- 1/2 cup of salted butter
- 3/4 cup of brown sugar
- 1 egg
- 1 1/4 cups of buckwheat flour
- 4 ounces of chocolate
- 1/2 cup of fresh or dried cranberries
- 1 teaspoon of baking soda
- Half a teaspoon of vanilla extract

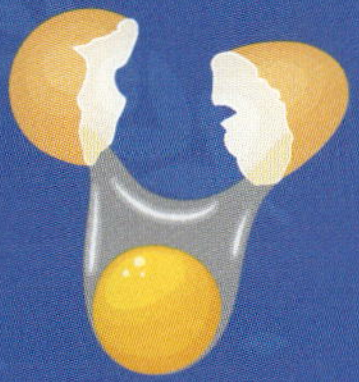

Let's cook!

- Heat oven to 400 degrees Fahrenheit (200 degrees Celsius).
- Put your butter and sugar in a bowl. Beat it until it is creamy.
- Beat in your egg and vanilla extract.
- Stir in your buckwheat flour, baking soda, chocolate, cranberries, and two tablespoons of cold water.
- Spoon your mixture onto a baking tray. Leave plenty of space between each spoonful.
- Bake for 15 to 20 minutes.

Allergies and Us

It is okay to feel worried after finding out you have a wheat allergy. However, having a wheat allergy does not mean you cannot enjoy delicious food.

Which wheat-free food are you most excited to try?

You can still safely eat a healthy balanced diet. Remember to check food labels and be careful what you order at restaurants. Ask a grown-up if you are not sure.

Glossary

carbohydrate food that contains sugar and starch

energy the power that makes living things able to move and live

ingredient a food product that is combined with other food products to make a particular dish

injects pushes a liquid into something using a needlelike object

reaction something done or felt in response to something else

source where something comes from

swelling becoming bigger than normal

symptoms signs of an illness that can be used to tell what is wrong with someone

whole grains types of seeds that have not been processed or changed

Index